Amish Weddings

Ellie's Homecoming
Book One

Samantha Bayarr

D1490563

Chapter 1

Ellie bounced little Katie lightly in her arms, trying to coax her back to sleep, while staring at the wedding invitation in her hand. Why had her *mamm* sent it when she knew Jonas had been her first and only love? Her *mamm* knew the history; knew that he'd made his choice to marry Hannah instead. It had broken Ellie's heart, but the real damage had already been done, and she hadn't realized it until weeks after she'd left the community. That afternoon she'd spent in the hayloft with Jonas trying to convince him to change his mind and leave the community with her had only resulted in the *boppli* she now held in her arms. But it had left her with more than that. She'd suffered heartache and shame, and in the end, made the difficult decision to raise the child on her own.

She thought Jonas would have married Hannah that very next month after she'd left, but instead had made her wait more than two years. Ellie had to wonder if he'd waited for her to return all that time, and when she hadn't, she supposed he'd given up on her.

Knowing Jonas had a right to know he had a daughter, this trip home was not going to be easy, but she was not going to break up his marriage if he was truly happy with Hannah.

Since she'd managed to keep little Katie a secret even from her *mamm,* as time went by, it became easier to keep it from her. She didn't expect that Jonas knew, or he'd likely have come looking for her. If *daed* were still alive, she'd not have dared to step foot back on the homestead, but *mamm* had been all alone after she'd left the community. Her twin brother, Eli and his wife, Lydia, who had married just before she'd left, were nearly ready to have their first child. *Mamm* had written her about her excitement over being a *grossmammi* in one of the many letters of correspondence to her in the time that she'd been away. She'd wished more than anything that she'd had the nerve to write in her return letter about little Katie, but she lost her nerve every time she began that letter. Now, as she sat at the train station waiting for the cab to take her home, she wished she'd said something—anything that would prepare her *mamm* for the shock that could hurt Katie.

Would *mamm* welcome another grandchild? Would her own brother refuse to allow little Katie to grow up alongside her new cousin? They were all questions that put fearful butterflies in the pit of her stomach. Not the happy fluttery kind she used to get when Jonas would kiss her. These were the ones that made her shake and shiver at the slightest autumn breeze that cooled the perspiration from her cheeks.

The bigger question on the forefront of her mind at the moment; the one that caused her much more anxiety than coming home with a *boppli* in her arms, was the wedding invitation. Hannah was her best friend, and Jonas had been the love of her life ever since they were old enough to walk and talk. But her decision to spend her *rumspringa* among the *Englischers* had been what had caused her to lose her best friend and her would-be husband forever.

Why couldn't Jonas have gone with her the way she'd begged him to? He'd threatened he would marry Hannah if she left, and she'd foolishly challenged him, hoping in the back of her mind he would follow her, run after her, and beg her to come back, or at the very least, wait for her.

He hadn't done anything but choose to marry Hannah just as he'd threatened, and it had broken her heart. Now, as she looked at his wedding invitation, she felt fresh hurt writhing in her gut, rolling around like hot coals in her *mamm's* old cook-stove.

Little Katie's breath hitched from crying so much; she hadn't liked the train ride, and it had upset her stomach so much she drooled a bit of milk on Ellie's shoulder. Her Mennonite cousin, Esther, had cried when they'd left the city. She'd taken Ellie into her home when she first realized she was pregnant. Esther had advised her to go home and tell Jonas about the baby then, but she was too concerned with being shunned by her strict Amish *familye*.

She wished she'd taken that advice.

Ellie closed her eyes against the warm, afternoon sun, remembering the last day she'd seen Jonas. Over the past couple of years, she'd tried to put that rainy afternoon in the barn out of her mind. She'd struggled to forget it, but every gurgle from little Katie brought that day fresh in her mind as if it was only yesterday. Never would she have dreamed things would go that far with her and Jonas. Afterward, it had been awkward. With the passion between them spent, Jonas quickly realized what a mistake it had been, and tried to make excuses for losing control of his emotions the way he had. Ellie had certainly taken it personally, believing he wished it had not happened.

She cuddled her daughter, knowing because of Katie, she could never regret that day. Her only regret had been in leaving the community, and it was too late to take it back now.

A taxi pulled up in front of the bench she rested on in front of the train station. His brakes squeaked as he came to a complete stop, and the tailpipe rattled and sputtered as if it might just fall off if he hit a bump in the road. Thick smoke trailed from the pipe, causing Ellie to rise from the bench and cough at the smell of exhaust. She covered little Katie's face with her blanket to shield her from the smell, as she motioned to the driver to get her bags that lay on the bench where she'd been sitting.

He snuffed out the butt of a cigar with a clunky brown shoe, and grunted as he bent down and grabbed for her bags. His button-down, short-sleeved Hawaiian shirt puckered at every button over the girth of his belly that protruded over the waist of his Bermuda shorts.

"You travel pretty light with that baby, Miss," he said as he picked up her bags. "You must not be planning on visiting long."

She nodded and forced a smile.

She hadn't thought about how long she would stay; she'd only thought about whether or not she'd be welcome. Fresh anxiety filled her as she watched the driver pick up the car seat and buckle it into the back seat as if he'd done it a thousand times for the passengers before her. Katie didn't even wake up as she strapped her in, and then tugged on the seat to make sure it was secure. Katie was oblivious to the trouble they could be walking into, and Ellie suddenly wondered why she was putting herself through all of this.

She kissed little Katie's soft cheek and buckled herself in next to the child, reminding herself she had to put away her own fears for the sake of her daughter. She and her father had a right to know one another, even if that meant Ellie, herself, had to endure a little pain to make it happen for them. Her life was no longer her own, and for that reason, she would do anything for her daughter.

Chapter 2

Before she was ready to face it, the taxi pulled into the driveway Ellie hadn't seen in over two years. She paused before getting out of the cab, looking out at the house she hadn't stepped foot in for the same amount of time. Maybe she was being silly, but the trees seemed to have grown several feet, and the grass seemed a little thicker, perhaps because her brother hadn't cut it as often as he should.

The cherry tree on the side yard that her *daed* always carefully pruned and babied had grown a little out of control. The cherries had been picked from the lower branches, indicating her *mamm* had likely used them for a few pies, or perhaps a few jars of preserves, but the rest remained on the top limbs of the large tree, where birds fought over the fruit. Her *daed* would have never let the tree get to that condition if he were still alive, but she supposed her *mamm* had done the best she could.

All was quiet, except the familiar squeak of the windmill near the barn. She listened to the constant click, click, click, as it turned in the slight breeze. Her *daed* had promised to fix it just before he'd died, and afterward, her *mamm* would not let her brother repair it. She knew it reminded her mother of her father, and she'd stated more than once that every time she heard it, she could hear his voice right along with it promising her he'd fix it just as soon as he had the time. With him growing weaker from the cancer that had consumed his liver, fixing the windmill had been the last thing on his mind. And now, as Ellie listened to it, the sound almost brought her the same comfort.

She lifted little Katie from her car seat and stepped out of the vehicle, closing the bulky door a little hard. The noise startled the birds, causing them to scatter from the cherry tree and squawk their annoyance with her. She giggled slightly remembering the day her *daed* had offered to pay her a whole dollar to be a scarecrow under the tree. She was only ten years old, and had wanted some candy at the store in town so badly; she'd stayed out there *cawing* almost all day, despite her brother making fun of her. The following day, she was so sore from flapping her arms to shoo away the birds, she told her *daed* she didn't want to be a scarecrow anymore, but he'd given her the dollar just as he'd promised.

After that, she decided it was easier to stick to gathering the eggs for the morning meal. From the time she'd been big enough to walk, *mamm* had trusted her with the chore; the chickens being her responsibility. But from that day on, she stuck to taking the extra eggs to their *Englisch* neighbors for the quarter they'd *tip* her for walking them over.

Ellie took in a deep breath and swallowed the lump in her throat. Now was not the time for remembering her *daed;* she needed to prepare herself for the possibility her *mamm* would not welcome her home.

The taxi driver had set her bags and Katie's car seat in the grassy area beside the gravel driveway. She handed him the money for the fare and asked him not to leave—just in case she wouldn't be staying.

Lifting her eyes toward the house, she noted the front porch was in need of sweeping, and the windows in need of washing. Had her *mamm* let things go to such an extent that she didn't even keep up with her regular chores anymore? Or perhaps her mother was ill and had not mentioned it in any of her letters. She knew her mother had still been slightly depressed when Ellie had decided to leave for her *rumspringa*, but the heartbroken woman had urged her to go anyway.

Her *mamm* had missed out on her own *rumspringa* because she had married her father at such a young age. She'd never regretted the decision. However, she'd still urged Ellie to explore the world a little before getting married to Jonas. Ellie sighed, wondering if she could use that as an argument in case her mother rejected little Katie. She knew it wasn't her mother's fault that she'd gotten pregnant, because it had happened before she'd left for her *rumspringa*.

Had Ellie known at the time she left that she was with child, she likely would not have gone. But after three months had passed, she found out the news. At that point, she worried about coming back to the community and finding Jonas had married Hannah, and knew it would break her heart that much more. And so she stayed away, and never said a word about it to her mother. Weeks had turned into months, and the months somehow got away from her, turning into years.

Jonas's wedding invitation was the first mention of him since she'd left. She'd made her *mamm* promise she would not discuss him in order to give Ellie the time she needed for her *rumspringa* without feeling guilty that she'd left him behind.

Not only that, her mother had reminded her of his threat, and told her that if he followed through with that threat he wasn't worth wasting any tears on. She told her daughter just before she left *"Don't shed any tears over anyone who wouldn't shed any for you."*

Her *mamm* was always wise like that, and full of advice for her, but taking her *rumspringa* was one bit of advice she wished she would've ignored.

It was too late for all of that now; the damage was done, and could not be undone.

Leaving her bags near the driveway, Ellie put Katie over her shoulder and walked up onto the wraparound porch of her childhood home. She sighed, pulling in a ragged breath as she lifted her hand to knock on the door. Before her knuckles met with the heavy wooden door, it flew open unexpectedly; her *mamm* standing before her with a surprised expression.

Ellie stood there staring at the woman, whose tired eyes darted between her and the little girl in her arms, and then back again to look at her straight on. Though her *mamm* had aged, the familiar look of *home* in her eyes was enough to bring tears to her eyes.

Her *mamm* stepped back after a moment's pause, as if to invite Ellie inside the house, but couldn't find her voice.

"You must be tired from the long journey from Ohio," the woman finally said, stumbling over her words.

She smiled nervously, avoiding asking about the baby.

Ellie stepped inside the house feeling suddenly very out of sorts in the place she used to call home.

Maybe this was a bad idea, she thought to herself. *But it's too late to turn back now, she's already seen her.*

Little Katie hiccupped and then began to cry, likely sensing her mother's nervousness. Ellie's *mamm* looked at her, and then held her arms out awkwardly toward the *boppli.* Ellie relinquished Katie into her *mamm's* arms, but still the woman had said nothing about her.

Ellie watched as her *mamm* cradled her daughter, jostling her slightly and cooing to her. She immediately stopped crying and she raised her gaze toward her own daughter.

Feeling terrified to even breathe, Ellie stood in front of her *mamm* paralyzed, feeling as if she'd just gotten caught stealing an extra cookie when she was five years old.

Her *mamm* looked back down into little Katie's face, her eyes wide open and looking at the woman. "If I'm not mistaken," she said to little Katie. "I think I'm your *grossmammi.*"

Ellie let out the breath she been holding in as if she'd never breathe again, blowing out a sigh of relief.

"*Jah,*" she said awkwardly. "She is *mei dochder.*"

Her *mamm* rolled her eyes upward, narrowing them as if she were thinking. "And I'm guessing by her age, she's Jonas's *dochder* as well."

"Jah, Mamm, she is," Ellie said.

"What do you plan to do about it?" her *mamm* asked in her matter-of-fact way.

"I wish I knew," Ellie said. "But I think my biggest worry right at the moment," she admitted, "is whether or not I should get my bags off the front lawn and bring them in."

Her *mamm* smiled, tears welling up in her eyes. She held her arms out to her daughter and pulled her close, kissing her hair. "*Wilkum* home, *dochder,*" she said. "*Wilkum* home."

Chapter 3

Jonas finished shaving, and then took a good hard look at himself in the small mirror in his bathroom. If something didn't change for him soon, if God didn't answer his prayer, this might be one of the last times he would ever shave his face in full again.

He'd thought many times about backing out of his pact with Hannah, but he most certainly didn't want to grow too old without the opportunity to start a family and be married. He couldn't help but feel that marrying her was not the right thing to do. Not when he still carried so much love for Ellie. They were supposed to be married and have a family— and grow old together. That was the plan his entire life. They likely would have celebrated an anniversary, and possibly the birth of a child by now if she hadn't left.

When she left, everything changed for him.

His future was about as unstable as a person's life could get. He was about to marry a woman he didn't love, and have a family with her. What had he been thinking when he'd agreed to such a thing?

He'd been grieving, that was for certain.

Grieving for the loss of the love of his life, and he'd agreed to such a plan hoping it would ease the pain, but it hadn't. It had only brought him new grief.

Was it fair to Hannah to keep it from her that he had sent for Ellie? He'd hoped that seeing her again would either give him the closure he desperately needed, or he would know once and for all that his love for her was still so genuine he couldn't live without her.

But what if she didn't come to see him? What if she decided to ignore the invitation and let him marry Hannah?

He dried his face and took one last look at his clean-shaven face.

At least then, I'll know for sure.

He went out to the kitchen of the house he'd built hoping his Ellie would return to him and marry him, suddenly realizing Hannah would soon be making this kitchen her own.

Pouring himself a cup of coffee, he stood at the window and stared out at the spot where he'd started a kitchen garden for Ellie, and the chickens that roamed the yard that she'd been so eager to raise. Everything about this house had been made with Ellie in mind, and now, another woman was about to invade those future dreams they'd shared so long ago.

Though Ellie had never spent a single minute at this house, there wasn't one part of it that didn't remind him of her. He'd laid awake many a night in the room he'd hoped to share with her, thinking about what their children would look like, and how many grandchildren would eventually fill the house with an equal amount of noise.

He felt sad as he thought about not having a little Ellie running around this house. He supposed he and Hannah might eventually grow their relationship enough to include a few children. But what if they didn't? He wasn't even certain if he was going to sleep in his own bed after the wedding. He knew the right thing to do would be to offer to sleep in one of the many rooms in the house until they got to know one another better, but he wasn't exactly eager to make the offer. She'd expect to be able to use the master bedroom. It would be her right to do so, but it hardly seemed fair to him. After all, it was *his* home that she was invading.

I suppose it will be her home too once we get married.

Lord, I'm not sure I'm ready for this. I pray you'll intervene and show me the right thing to do. I don't want to hurt Hannah, but you know my heart, Lord. You know I'll never be able to love Hannah the way I love Ellie.

An unexpected tear streamed down his cheek and he swiped at it angrily. Before the day was through, he had to tell Hannah the truth, whether Ellie returned or not.

He just wasn't ready to put away his feelings and marry another woman, no matter how practical it seemed.

His heart just wasn't in it.

Chapter 4

Fifteen-year-old Rachel went running into the house, yelling for her sister. She ran up the stairs calling for her, when the sound of her mother's voice stopped her.

"Don't run in the haus!" her *mamm's* memory scolded her.

Rachel ignored her mother's haunting voice that came from deep within her grieving heart, continuing to run up the remainder of the stairs until she found her sister. She paused to watch Hannah making the beds with the fresh linens from the clothesline. Her sister looked so much like their *mamm* she could almost trick her mind into believing the woman had not recently gone to Heaven, but she had, and Hannah had tried to fill the gap for her as best she could.

She ignored the thought of her *mamm* the same as she had for close to two years since she'd been gone.

"You'll never guess who's back!" she said, gasping for breath.

Hannah waited impatiently just the way her *mamm* would have, waiting for her little sister to catch her breath before answering.

"Our cousins just told me your old friend, Ellie, is here visiting her *mamm,* and she's brought a *boppli* with her!"

Hannah dropped the pillow onto the bed and grabbed her sister by her shoulders, forcing her to look her in the eye. "Tell me everything!" she demanded, sitting on the partially-made bed. "How old is the *boppli*? Is it a boy or a girl? Who is she married to? Did she bring her husband with her?"

"Wait a minute; that's too many questions! They said she was here by herself," Rachel said. "They don't think she's married, and she has a little girl about eighteen months old. Almost certain it's her *boppli*. They did say she looks like an *Englischer*."

Hannah stood up and went over to the second-floor window and stared out as she did the math in her head. The timing of Ellie's absence from the community suggested she'd gotten pregnant just before leaving, or perhaps within days after arriving in Ohio. If before, was there a chance her Jonas was the *vadder?* If not, that could only mean she'd been untrue to Jonas and had someone waiting for her in Ohio.

Hannah sucked in her breath and swallowed hard at the realization. It was gossip, she knew, but she *had* to know more.

"Why is she here?" she asked, picking up the quilt and smoothing it over the bed.

Rachel picked up the other end and helped her finish making their parent's bed. "They said her *mamm* sent her an invitation to your wedding. Rumor has it that Jonas gave it to her to send!"

"He never said anything to me about inviting her! Why would she want to come to my wedding when she hasn't spoken one word to me in more than two years?"

"To see Jonas! Do you suppose she's here to get him back?" Rachel asked.

Hannah tossed the pillows onto the bed, and Rachel straightened them.

"I don't think I want to wait around to find out!" she said, crossing to the bedroom window and looking out at the neighboring farm where her friend used to live, and was now visiting.

There used to be a time when she and Ellie would meet each other halfway in the cornfield. They would run around in the maze of rows for hours, catching fireflies and giggling. They didn't have a care in the world then.

Now, she'd invested two years of her life into Jonas, waiting for him to propose.

If Jonas was the father of Ellie's baby, he would call off the wedding for sure and for certain. She had to go over there and confront her friend. She had to know the truth, even if it ruined her life.

Hannah marched up the steps to the Yoder house and knocked on the door boldly, intending to put a stop to the gossip before it started. The Widow Yoder answered the door; a little girl dressed in *Englisch* clothing in her arms.

"Hannah," she greeted her daughter's friend. "*Wie ghetts?* I haven't seen you for a long time. Would you like to come in?"

Hannah looked deeply into the child's little face noting the same features of her betrothed. Her heart sank at the thought of such a beautiful little gift from *Gott* could cause the destruction of her marriage.

"I came to see Ellie," she said, unable to take her eyes off the *boppli.* "Is she here?"

"I sent her in town to run a few errands for me," Widow Yoder said. "You're *wilkum* to stay and wait for her if you'd like.

She'd seen all she'd needed to see, but it wouldn't seem polite to turn down an invitation from a neighbor. She had truly missed sitting in *Frau*

Yoder's kitchen eating cookies with her friend. But those days were gone. Things had changed; and not for the better. She shook inside as she walked into the home she hadn't been in for more than a handful of times since Ellie's departure. There was a time when her own ma'am could not pry her away, but now she would do almost anything to get out of having to go inside and face what was before her. How was it that she'd become part of a triangle with her own best friend?

Had Jonas used her all this time to get over Ellie? She was about to be dumped, and for a fleeting moment, she wasn't sure if she truly cared. It was almost more of a relief to her. She'd been stricken with so much guilt for having taken Ellie's place in Jonas's life all this time. She had known all along that his heart truly remained with Ellie, and that she had been his second choice.

She sat down on the settee very methodically. Before she realized, Frau Yoder had begun to fuss about something and she hadn't been paying attention. Lost in her own world, Hannah was suddenly holding Ellie's child.

"I'll just be a minute," *Frau* Yoder called over her shoulder to Hannah. I don't want my cookies to burn.

Hannah focused on the little girl sitting happily on her lap. The little girl smiled, putting a lump in Hannah's throat.

"What is your name, little one?" Hannah asked.

Frau Yoder overheard her. "Her name is Katie," she said from the kitchen.

"She looks so much like Ellie when we were younger," Hannah said loud enough for the widow Yoder to hear her.

"She certainly was a surprise," the woman said. "Did Ellie write you about her?"

"*Nee*," Hannah said. "I haven't gotten a single letter from Ellie since she left for her *rumspringa*. I'll bet her father is very proud of her," Hannah said, fishing for information. "Did Ellie bring her husband along on this trip?"

"I'm sure when Ellie returns from town, the two of you can catch up and she'll tell you all about it," *Frau* Yoder answered, bringing a plate of warm cookies from the kitchen on a tray with two teacups and a ceramic pot of tea.

Hannah knew better than to continue to pry, but she had to admit she was eager for Ellie to return so she could get the truth even though she knew it already. Mostly in the way *Frau* Yoder was avoiding answers that were easy. It was all in what she *wasn't* saying that made Hannah realize she was trying very hard to keep the truth from her.

It was obvious to Hannah that Jonas was this child's father; she looked just like him and had his eyes. But the two of them had vowed to save themselves for their wedding night; had she been alone in that vow?

Katie leaned against Hannah's unyielding frame and yawned, looking up at her with a pair of blue eyes that mirrored Jonas's. She'd anticipated having *kinner* with him, and had often wondered what his offspring would look like.

Now she knew.

Hannah felt the weight of the *boppli* shift as she slumped against her, falling into a deep sleep. She cradled the child, leaning down and smelling her hair. She still had that *baby smell.*

The child trusted her enough to fall asleep in her arms, and it made her regret some of the things she was already feeling. They were selfish feelings; feelings that would only benefit her, when she should be thinking of the child.

Jonas will be able to see this child if she was his, even if he married her instead of Ellie. Hannah would make sure of it. She cared enough about Jonas to let him do his own choosing. It was true, she had not allowed herself to love him the way that a wife should, but she hadn't dared give him her whole heart, for fear Ellie would come back and her heart would be broken.

Now, it would seem that time had come.

Chapter 5

Ellie stood in front of the shops on Main Street, her *mamm's* quilt in her arms. She'd asked her to take it into the shop for a customer who was waiting on it, but Ellie knew it was so her mother could spend some time with Katie. She didn't mind running her *mamm's* errands, and she was happy that she wanted to spend time with little Katie. She hoped they would bond so her child could have a grandmother.

She walked into the shop, anticipating a welcome from Mary, the shop owner, but instead, ran into Jonas. With the quilt in front of her face, she was unable to see where she was going, and ran smack into him!

Dropping her *mamm's* quilt, she bent to pick it up, and bumped heads with Jonas. Was this a cruel joke?

"I'm sorry," he said, staring.

She placed her hand on her forehead and bent over to pick up the quilt, watching to be sure he didn't bend a second time and bump her again.

"I'm so glad I ran into you," he said, rubbing his head. "Not literally, but you know what I meant."

She forced a weak smile, and he flashed her the same swaggering smile that used to make her melt at the sight of it. She wasn't surprised that it had the same effect on her even now. It unnerved her that his smile could still make her swoon.

"Did you get the invitation?" he asked awkwardly.

She pulled the wadded quilt close to her and blew at the hair that hung over her face so she could look him in the eye.

She was too stunned to answer.

"I took an invitation to your *mamm* so she could forward it to you since I didn't have an address for you," he said with confidence.

"Why would you want *me* at your wedding to Hannah?"

His look softened, and he fumbled with the spools of white and blue thread in his hand. "I was hoping to see you once more before I…"

His voice trailed off, and anger set in her.

"So you could what?" she asked, trying to be quiet, despite her temper flaring. "So you could break my heart one last time before you marry my best friend?"

"It's not like that, Ellie," he said softly.

"You told me you were going to marry her when I left here more than two years ago, and now you've made her wait all this time, and you're still not sure?"

"It's not like that, Ellie," he said a little louder. "I promise you it isn't. Hannah doesn't love me any more than I love her!"

Ellie nearly dropped the quilt. Did this change anything, or did it only complicate things?

"How do you know she doesn't love you?"

She wished she hadn't asked. She wished she could walk away. Lord help her, she still loved him, and if there was even a semblance of a chance she could have him back in her life, she would listen to what he had to say.

"Neither of us is getting any younger, and we've talked about this. We're *gut* friends, but we don't love each other like—well, not with the sort of love and passion you and I had."

Ellie had silently paid for that *passion,* and now her daughter would too if she didn't at least give her father a chance to know her. But she would not get between Jonas and Hannah no matter how much she wanted to be a family with Jonas.

"What if you're wrong about Hannah? You can't break her heart."

"From the talks we've had, I don't think her heart would be broken if I didn't marry her. You know I've always loved you, Ellie, and thought you and I would get married."

Ellie walked toward the counter when she noticed the store owner go to the back room. She set the quilt on the counter and turned around, realizing Jonas was on her heels.

"You made up my mind when you threatened to marry my best friend simply because I wanted to enjoy my *rumspringa!"*

"I only said that because I was hoping it would make you stay. Then when you told me to go ahead and marry her, I thought you didn't love me anymore."

Mary came back to the counter, her eyes lighting up when she saw Ellie. The older woman pulled her into a hug. "I'm so glad to see you, Ellie. You're so grown up!"

Ellie smiled, realizing Jonas had walked back to get the notions he'd set down.

"Your mother told me you were coming for a visit."

Her *mamm* had been friends with the *Englisch* woman for as long as Ellie could remember, and had been bringing her quilts to sell ever since *daed* had died. She'd needed the income, and the older woman who owned the shop had been very helpful in helping her *mamm* make enough money to live off.

She picked up the quilt. "My customer is going to love this new quilt. It turned out better than I thought it would. She'd brought me a hand-drawn design, and I wasn't sure how your mother was going to pull it off, but she did a beautiful job!"

"Thank you, I'll be sure to pass that on to her."

The woman handed her a receipt for the quilt, and Ellie walked toward the door, intending to end the conversation between herself and Jonas, but he caught her gently by the arm and stopped her.

"Let me pay for *mei mamm's* things and give me a few minutes, please? I'd like to finish our talk."

Ellie reluctantly nodded, though she thought they'd said all there was to say. He was marrying her best friend, and nothing would ever be the same again.

Seconds ticked by in her head as she waited for him, though they seemed like hours. She didn't want to be there; it made her feel uncomfortable. Almost as if she worried the old woman would tattle on her to her mother like she was a child in trouble. Why had being back home suddenly made her feel like a child again? She was a grown woman with a child of her own, and here she was shaking in her shoes.

It was too late for the two of them to talk, wasn't it? Her heart felt heavy, and her throat constricted. She would not cry over him again. She had steeled her emotions against this, and it had been a hard lesson. Why, then, was she so willing to go back to that place in her life where he could hurt her? Being in his presence made her feel vulnerable, and she'd worked hard to be strong for little Katie's sake.

Ah, Katie.

That's who she would endure this for. Even if he rejected her all over again, Ellie would give him a chance—for her daughter's sake.

Chapter 6

Ellie stood outside the quilt shop, lifting her face to the sky and breathing a simple prayer.

Lord, please show me if I'm doing the right thing by speaking with Jonas. I still love him. He's the love of my life and the man I believed you had for me. Remove the guilt from my heart, Lord, if it is not a warning from you, but a trick from the enemy. If I am not to have him in my life, please remove the love in my heart that I have for him. Help me not to be selfish, but to put the needs of my friend, Hannah, before my own. If it is your will, please bring Jonas back to me if he's truly in love with me, not just for my daughter's sake.

No sooner had she finished speaking her prayer in her mind and in her heart, than Jonas exited the quilt shop and stood quietly beside her.

~~~~

"Hey, Rachel, isn't that Jonas with that *Englisch* woman over there in front of the quilt shop?"

Rachel pulled her cousin, Lydia, behind a row of cars parked in front of the meters downtown. "Let's spy on him for *mei schweschder!*"

Both girls giggled, and followed as the pair walked the opposite direction toward the park.

"What do you suppose he's up to?" Lydia asked quietly, as they ducked behind another car when the woman turned around.

"Wait a minute!" Rachel said, entirely too loud. "That looks like Ellie! What is he doing with her? Wait till Hannah finds out!"

~~~~

Ellie and Jonas stood in front of the fountain they'd spent many hours near when they courted, talking over future plans, and sharing too many kisses to count. It seemed only natural they would migrate there now.

"You know I didn't want things to be this way"' he said. "I hoped we'd be married and maybe with a *boppli* on the way."

Ellie's face turned red for two reasons; first, because she was keeping the baby a secret from him, and two, it brought to mind that steamy afternoon they'd had in the barn with wild abandon.

"*Ach,* I didn't mean to speak in such a forward manner," he said.

Ellie drew her hands up to her warm cheeks. Had he noticed the redness?

She struggled to speak, wanting to tell him everything about Katie, but for some reason she couldn't find her voice. Not only was she unable to speak the words he needed to hear, she had suddenly realized it may not be the right time. She did not want him coming back to her simply for little Katie. His relationship with his daughter would have to be completely separate, but if he was to return to her and be one with her, he needed to do it without knowing about Katie first. The last thing she wanted was for him to ask to marry her out of obligation. She still loved him as much as she ever did, if not more now because of Katie, and she needed to be sure his love for her was genuine.

"I only meant," he continued. "That I had hope for a future with you. Until you left, I always thought we'd be married."

"Why didn't you come after me?" She asked

"When you left, I thought you didn't love me anymore, because when I told you I would marry Hannah, you told me to go ahead and marry her. I don't think you understand how much that hurt me."

"I didn't think you'd go through with such a thing. I was young and stupid and angry," she said. "I was so hurt by your threat that I thought, if you

were capable of doing it, then I didn't want anything
to do with you. I thought you no longer loved me."

He chuckled lightheartedly, trying to make
light of an awkward situation. "It sounds as if we
both had the wrong idea about each other. But the
fact still remains, I still love you, and if you love me,
I don't want to marry Hannah simply to be married. I
have a promise to marry her, that's all. We made a
promise that if neither of us was married in two
years, we would marry each other and start a
familye. But that's not what I want. I want to have a
familye with you. I love you. I've always loved you.
I could never love anyone but you."

Ellie was tempted to throw her arms around
his neck and pick up just where they'd left off, but
she had her child to think about now. What if he
changed his mind once he saw Katie? She would be
devastated, to say the least. How could she tell him
now in this moment? She'd waited this long. A few
more days couldn't possibly hurt anything.

"When do the two years expire?"

Jonas looked down at his feet, unable to look
her in the eye. "On the eve of our wedding. Two
days from now."

Ellie thought back to the wedding invitation
she received. They were to be married on Thursday,
a traditional Amish wedding day. Her heart sank at
the realization that Jonas must have already taken
the baptism. She had not. He would not be able to

marry her without being shunned, and knowing Jonas, he would not be able to live with that. Neither would she.

Ellie collapsed onto the park bench and stared into the water shower the fountain was making. How could she agreed to marry him now when it would ruin his standing in the community?

He sat beside her, and stared equally at the fountain, unsure of what to say to her. How could he convince her of his love after what he just confessed to her? Really, he wouldn't blame her if she never wanted to speak to him again. He knew he'd hurt her not once, but twice. He'd avoided taking the baptism until the last minute, knowing he would have to confess his love for Ellie. Was he hoping Ellie would get him out of this jam?

Certainly, he didn't want to have to confess his sin of passion with Ellie to the bishop, but that was no reason not to marry Hannah. He fully intended to make good on his commitment to Hannah if it was Ellie's wish that he do so, but he prayed heavily that was not the case. The confession, he knew, was merely an excuse. He loved Ellie so much his heart ached just sitting next to her. It took every ounce of his strength not to pull her into his arms and beg her to marry him. But he would not put pressure on her, nor would he try to influence her decision in anyway. He stated the facts to her, and that's all he could do. The rest was up to her.

Ellie rested her head on Jonas's shoulder, feelings of helplessness overtaking her. He wrapped his arm around her and cradled her, making her feel like that same young girl who fell in love with him an entire lifetime ago. Had things really changed that much for them? They had a bond, it seemed, that was unbreakable no matter what the circumstances. But was it really? Jonas was days away from marrying another woman, and he had no idea he and Ellie had a child together. Had she made a mistake in coming home?

"I'm afraid it might be too late for us," she finally said.

She stood up, not wanting to leave him, but she promised her *mamm* she wouldn't be long.

"I have to go," she said abruptly.

She knew if she didn't leave now, she would never be able to leave his side. She would not be the one to make this decision; she could not make it no matter how much she wanted to. She had a million things rolling in her head at the moment, her head swimming with emotion. But she knew that to allow her emotions to make her decision could cause a lot of unnecessary hurt. How funny it was to her that she longed to hear those words from him for so long, but now that he'd said them, she wasn't sure if she could accept them. Had she grown up a little too fast? She knew time was short, as the wedding was only a few days away, but that was no reason to make a hasty decision that could hurt her friend. Did she have a right to be so selfish as to take away Hannah's betrothed?

Jonas stood up, pulling her hands into his. "Please don't go," he begged her.

She looked into his eyes, knowing that all she wanted was to be able to look into them for the rest of her life. If he kissed her now, she knew there would be no turning back.

Before she could break free from him, he pulled her into a passionate embrace, pressing his lips to hers, his love for her all too evident. Her eyes drifted closed as she felt his lips on hers, sweeping across them with the passion she longed to feel once again. She deepened the kiss, unable to hold back her love for him. Concern for Hannah had left her; all her thoughts were now consumed by the passion of Jonas's embrace.

She was not ready to let him go. God help her, she loved this man with every fiber of her being. He was a part of her. He always would be. Even despite their separation, she'd felt his presence across the vast miles that had separated them for more than two years. Time and distance had not separated them; it had not destroyed the love they had for one another.

Nothing, not even Hannah, could ever get between them.

Chapter 7

Ellie straightened up on the buggy seat, inching away from Jonas's embrace as they entered the long driveway that led to her childhood home. She had good news for her mother about Jonas's proposal, but she would not present him in an inappropriate light. She knew her *mamm* already had misgivings about him because of the child she'd brought home with her, and if she could help it, she would make Jonas look like a shiny new penny in order to sell her *mamm* on the idea things would be alright with them.

Her biggest worry now was to get through introducing Jonas to his daughter, and hope they took to one another. Little Katie had been a good baby, and had taken to her *mamm* quite easily, but she'd not been around any men except Cousin Henry, and she cried whenever he spoke in his deep voice.

Ellie knew there would be no preparing him to meet little Katie, and so she hadn't said a word the entire trip back home. She'd simply enjoyed having his arm around her and the security that came with it. She hadn't even thought about what she was going to say to him, but merely assumed the situation would take care of itself. Knowing what a kindhearted man he was, and how much he had just told her he wanted children with her, she almost couldn't wait for him to see the child they already had.

Jonas parked the buggy near the porch, and hopped out to help her down. Putting his hands around her waist, Jonas looked as though he would kiss her, but Ellie backed away. "Not in front of the *haus*," she warned him. "I don't want *Mamm* to get the wrong impression."

He smiled that same smile that always melted her heart. "I understand. Let's give her the good news first."

"What exactly is that news?" She asked curiously.

His expression fell. "Was I wrong, or did you agree to marry me back there in the park? I hope that kiss meant more to you than just a casual flirtation."

"Of course it did, but I suppose I hadn't realized that you'd officially asked me," she admitted. "I didn't want to assume anything."

He raised an eyebrow over his blue eyes. "I thought that kiss said it all, didn't it?"

She smiled happily, feeling even more giddy than ever.

"I believe it did."

They headed up the steps of the porch when the front door flung open. Hannah stood in the doorway, anger clouding her expression. Ellie looked around her for any sign of her *mamm* and little Katie, but Hannah was the only one there.

"Ellie, it's so nice to see you again," Hannah said.

Ellie wasn't convinced she was all that happy to see her, and fear entered her mind. Surely if Hannah was visiting with her *mamm*, then she also knew about little Katie. Would she open her mouth before she had a chance to introduce the child to Jonas? By the look on her face, she could tell she knew. Ellie walked up the remaining steps toward her friend, pulling her into an awkward embrace.

"I've missed you so much!" Ellie said to her.

Hannah looked between Ellie and Jonas, her jaw clenching from the tension between the three of them.

"I'd love to stay and visit, but I've been here waiting for so long, I just don't have any more time to spare; we'll have to *catch up* later. Please take me home, Jonas," Hannah said suddenly, slipping her arm in the crook of his elbow. "I have a lot to prepare for our wedding." She turned to Ellie. "You'll be there, won't you? At our wedding?"

Ellie couldn't mutter a word, but forced a smile. It was better coming from Jonas; it was his mess, and he'd have to get himself out of it. She could see by Hannah's mannerisms that she was not happy to see the two of them together, and she didn't want to be in the middle of it.

"Hannah, we need to talk," Jonas said grabbing her hand. He walked down the steps of the porch hand-in-hand with Hannah, but looked over his shoulder to flash Ellie a sorrowful look.

Ellie stood on the porch of her childhood home watching the love of her life walk away with her best friend. Hadn't he just proposed marriage to her? Yet here he was leaving with Hannah. She watched him assist Hannah into his buggy, looking up one last time in her direction before driving away.

What had just happened? Her world felt suddenly very small; her worry growing by leaps and bounds. No matter how much she tried to convince herself Jonas was going to let Hannah down easily, she just wasn't able to.

She walked into the house, determined that she would drown her sorrows in hugs from the child they shared, and wait for Jonas to come back. She hadn't even had a chance to introduce him to his daughter, and now he was gone. They were also going to break the news to her *mamm,* but now, she feared saying a word to her mother for fear it would not come to pass.

What if he never returned? Would she be any worse off than she was now? She'd thought Hannah and Jonas had been married all this time, and had shouldered the responsibility of little Katie alone.

Then her mind drifted to the passionate kiss they'd shared out in public in the park, without any reservations about anyone seeing them. It was that same passion that had brought Katie into this world, and now, it could be the last thing she remembered about him. It would stick with her in the same manner as the pregnancy had. Even little Katie was a constant reminder of the loss she'd experienced.

Ellie hadn't missed the look of guilt on Jonas's face as he drove off with Hannah. If he chose her friend a second time, it would crush her. What had she been thinking, getting involved in such a triangle of passion with Jonas a second time? Hadn't she learned her lesson the first time?

Walking into her childhood room, she went to her daughter, who slept peacefully in the same crib she'd slept in as a child. Her *mamm* must have dragged it in from the spare room where it had always been waiting for the grandchildren her parents had talked about so eagerly before her father's untimely death.

She smoothed her hand over Katie's blonde curls that reminded her of Jonas's.

Apparently, she hadn't learned her lesson at all.

Chapter 8

Jonas steered his buggy into the neighboring driveway, gathering his thoughts to prepare Hannah for a gentle let-down. He didn't want to hurt her; she'd become very close to him, and he considered her a cherished friend. But after seeing Ellie again, and the kiss they shared, all he had on his mind was marrying her before she had a chance to get away from him again. He'd been a fool to let her go, and he'd been an even bigger fool to think he could forget her if he married Hannah.

He was both angry and annoyed with Hannah for interrupting what could have turned out to be his engagement dinner with Ellie. But he supposed he shouldn't have that yet until he was no longer engaged to Hannah.

Hannah sighed as he pulled the buggy up to the barn behind her house. She knew what was coming; she knew Jonas was quiet the five minutes it took for him to get her home because he had breaking up with her on his mind, and didn't quite know how he intended to word it. But why should she suffer just because Ellie was back? Ellie didn't have any claim on Jonas any longer. He was *her* betrothed; Ellie had given up any claim she had on him the day she left the community and told him to marry her instead. Now, after all this time, did she really have that kind of power to ruin Hannah's life? It was true, she didn't love Jonas the way Ellie most likely did, but she still had a strong bond with the man; she wouldn't have agreed to marry him if she didn't. Most of all, she had his word he'd marry her; Ellie didn't have that.

"I think you have the right to know that I had a long talk with Ellie, and it seems maybe our business with one another isn't exactly finished, and I made the mistake once before thinking it was. I don't want to hurt you, but I've made this mistake once already. I don't intend to make the same mistake twice. I really care about you, Hannah, honest I do, but I think we should wait to marry until I've sorted all this out. I pray that you will understand, because the last thing I want to do is hurt you, especially if I decide not to marry you at all."

"If you intend to marry Ellie," Hannah said. "Please tell me now, and spare me the details."

"If honesty is what you seek," Jonas said. "Then I will be honest with you and tell you that I've asked Ellie to marry me once again."

"You asked Ellie to marry you when you were still betrothed to me? How could you humiliate me like that? Before the end of the day, the entire community will know what you've done!"

Jonas was distraught. He didn't know how to handle the hysterical woman, and he wasn't liking it one bit. If she didn't calm down, her dad would be out in the yard removing him from his property before he had a chance to fully explain things to Hannah. He was trying not to hurt her, but he wasn't doing a very good job of it.

"If you're marrying Ellie only for the *boppli*, we can have *kinner* of our own soon," Hannah tried bargaining with him.

Jonas looked shocked.

Didn't he know? If Ellie hadn't told him about Katie, perhaps she was not his biological child after all. In which case, she may just be in the market for a father for her child.

If Hannah had any say in the matter, that was not going to happen.

"Ellie has a *boppli*?" He uttered the word in almost a whisper, and his eyes had a far-off look in them.

"She didn't tell you she has a *boppli*?"

Jonas shook his head, his expression still blank.

"Are you sure you want to get mixed up with Ellie again; especially if she's keeping such a big secret from you? It seems to me she's only seeking a *vadder* for her *boppli*, and you're her target!"

Was this all a cruel joke at his expense? Why hadn't she told him about the child? Was she going to wait until after they were married and then spring it on him? Surely she was not that kind of woman! But then again, if she had a child, perhaps she was already married once before, or perhaps she was still married. Worse than that, did Ellie have a child out of wedlock? If she did, then perhaps their time of intimacy before she left the community must not have been the only time. Was she that kind of girl? He would have never thought so, but if she truly had a child of her own, what else was she capable of? By his definition, keeping such a thing from him was just as bad as lying to him. He had to know the truth, no matter how bad it was.

"Hannah, I'm sorry," he said. "But I have to go talk to Ellie and find out if what you say is true."

Hannah began to cry. To think all this time, she thought Jonas was an honorable man. She was obviously wrong about him, that he could be so fickle that he would go back to Ellie after all she'd done to both of them. She'd broken both their hearts when she left the community, and now it would seem she had returned to do more of the same.

"Hannah, please don't cry. I still cared deeply for you, but I have to know that you and I are not making a big mistake by marrying one another just for convenience."

Convenience was the exact reason she was marrying him, and she'd come to terms with that, and was okay with it. She knew what her prospects were at her age, and in the community in which they resided, and they were next to none if not none altogether. She'd accepted it. She'd come to terms with it. And now, he was taking even that away from her. Ellie had a child by whatever means that child came into this world, but Hannah, it would seem, would never have any. She'd been foolish to trust Jonas, especially since she knew he was on the rebound from Ellie. She knew he would never love her as much as he loved Ellie, and she accepted that.

Why had she let Jonas make such a fool of her?

"I'm sorry Jonas," she said, gritting her teeth. "But you made a vow to marry me, and I expect you to honor that vow. If you don't, you leave me no other choice but to have *mei daed* go to the bishop."

Sadly, she knew she didn't have a leg to stand on with the bishop since Jonas had not taken the baptism yet, but she was not above making the threat. She, herself, felt threatened at the moment, and desperation had taken hold of her.

He assisted her out of his buggy. I'm sorry it has to be this way, Hannah" he said. "I understand you feel the need to do what you said, but I have to do what I have to do as well. Perhaps when this is over, we can still be friends, no matter what the outcome."

Hannah wiped her tears and sniffled. "Somehow, I find that hard to believe."

Jonas hopped back in his buggy, guilt tearing at him. He hated to leave Hannah in the condition she was in, but the only thing he had on his mind was finding out about Ellie's baby.

Chapter 9

Hannah walked over to Ellie's house, knowing she was taking a risk, but she felt she couldn't just stand around and wait for her life to crumble around her. Though the sun was still low in the sky, it was already promising to be a very hot day. Birds chirped and squirrels skittered around the trees in her path, but she couldn't find her usual joy in any of it. Her heart felt heavy, and she was torn between doing what was right, and doing what was right for *her*.

Since she hadn't heard back from Jonas, she could only assume that he'd had a talk with Ellie last night after he left her, and the two of them had made plans to marry. She knew that if his plans were already made, there would be little that she could do to stop them, however, she knew she would regret it if she didn't at least try.

She stepped up cautiously on to Ellie's porch, where she was playing with her daughter.

Ellie forced a smile, wondering why Hannah was back. "Good morning," she said.

"I'm sure I'm the last person you want to see right now," Hannah said. "But I need to know what happened between you and Jonas when he came back here last night."

"He was here, but I was asleep," she said. "My *mamm* told me he was here but she didn't want to disturb me, since I was overtired from my trip here. After the two of you left yesterday, I went upstairs to take Katie for a little nap, and I fell asleep with her. I think it was a good thing I was asleep when he showed up, because it gave me more time to think about the situation."

"Ellie, if you're here to break up my wedding so that you can get Jonas back, and make him the *vadder* of your *boppli*, I'm asking you to turn around and go back to your cousin's house in Ohio!"

Ellie's heart jumped behind her rib cage at her friend's comment. Either Hannah felt extremely threatened by her presence there, or it was time she faced the reality that she and Hannah were just not friends anymore. She had not yet had the opportunity to speak with Jonas and tell him about Katie, and so she kept her mouth shut about the subject. Besides, she knew Hannah would never understand her dilemma, and even if she did, it didn't seem that she would care. Their friendship had obviously come to an end a long time ago without her realizing it.

It would seem Ellie had outgrown her.

"I don't owe you an explanation," Ellie said, defending herself. "And I would appreciate it if you would stay out of my personal business. You have no business and no right to come here talking with my mother trying to get information from her while I was gone yesterday."

"That's not how it started out," Hannah said. "I came over here because I heard you were in Town. That's all."

Ellie shook her head. "Your cousins saw me get off the train. They had a clear view to see that I had a child with me. After seeing me, they ran back and told you everything, and that's when you decided you needed to come and see for yourself."

"I didn't have to see for myself the kiss between you and *my betrothed* to know that it really happened—and in public!"

"I remember how things work around here. And I know you, Hannah. You couldn't wait to get information that would be the top gossip in the community. You and your cousins always did talk about anything and everything, and what you didn't know for fact, you would make up the details."

"Are you accusing me of being a gossip?" Hannah asked with a huff.

Ellie pursed her lips, and cast her eyes downward. It was obvious someone had seen her and Jonas in the park, and the steamy kisses they'd shared. But she was not going to let her friend suck her into the drama of the community. It had been one of the reasons she had wanted to venture out on her own. She needed to see if people outside of the community were the same, or if there were differences. Unfortunately, she'd discovered that they could sometimes be even more harsh.

Hannah watched Ellie play with her child, and couldn't help but feel a twinge of envy. If Ellie was successful in taking away her only chance to marry, then she would be childless. She was angry, and rightly so. She and Ellie had been friends for many years, but she'd always envied her. Things seemed to come easily for Ellie, whereas Hannah always seemed to struggle with everything.

Frau Yoder walked out onto the porch with a pitcher filled with lemonade and a couple of glasses, along with a plate of whoopie pies on a tray. She set the tray on the little table between the two friends, and picked up Katie, walking into the house with her without saying a word to either of them. It was obvious that her mother did not approve of their heated conversation out on the porch, but surely she had to know that the two of them needed to iron out their differences once and for all.

Ellie felt discouraged as she poured two glasses of lemonade, handing one to Hannah. She offered her a whoopie pie, but she shook her head without even looking at her. Putting the plate back on the tray, Ellie sighed, wondering if the two of

them would ever see eye to eye on anything ever
again.

"This bickering is getting us nowhere," Ellie
said. "If Jonas is truly happy with you, and truly
wants to marry you, then I wish you both the best.
However, I came here to speak my piece to Jonas,
and I intend to do just that. If he decides otherwise
after hearing what I have to say, then that is up to
him and not either of us."

Hannah slammed down her glass of
lemonade onto the tray and furrowed her brow. "If
you intend to pass that child off as belonging to
Jonas, I'm going to have a say in it!"

Ellie stood up, placing her glass onto the tray,
and turned to her friend. "I believe our conversation
here is done. In fact, I think all future conversations
between us are over as well. I thought we could pick
up where we left off with our friendship, but I was
wrong. I think our circumstances have caused us to
outgrow each other."

Hannah stood, determined to have the last
word. "If you think I'm going to stand by helplessly
while you destroy my life, I'm afraid I can't do that.
Jonas made a promise to me, and I intend to make
him keep his commitment to me, and that includes
marrying me—not you!"

Ellie turned toward the door intending to
leave it at that, but changed her mind. She was not
going to let Hannah bully her into letting go of

Jonas. She'd come this far to offer him his child, and that's just what she intended to do. "I will leave that decision up to Jonas!"

Hannah turned back. "There's nothing more for him to decide. He asked me to marry him, and we will be married in two days."

"He asked me too!" she shot back.

Ellie walked into the house and shut the door before Hannah could say another word.

Chapter 10

Hannah walked back home, feeling anger and resentment rise up in her. Was she destined to remain merely the midwife for the community since her *mamm* had passed away? There had been no one else in the community with the amount of experience she had since she'd always gone with her *mamm* to assist, and with her gone, Hannah had naturally taken over the position. She was always delivering others' *bopplin,* and now, it would seem she would never be able to have a *boppli* of her own.

She refused to accept that was to be her destiny. It wasn't what she'd prayed for. Jonas had been the answer to those prayers, hadn't he?

She kicked at a stone on the gravel, country road. Since she'd walked straight out from Ellie's house and down the driveway without thinking, she was now on the road, having to go around. With the fence along the road, there would be no cutting through the way she usually did. She'd gotten over there by cutting through the field, and now out on the road, it would be a long walk home. Wishing she'd worn her black, over-bonnet to shield her eyes from the sun, she lifted a hand, holding it there for a minute, as she squinted to see a bird's nest. Even the birds, it seemed, had wee ones of their own.

Was that the only reason she had agreed to marry Jonas?

She'd spent the last year forcing a courtship with him, knowing she had feelings that amounted to little more than friendship for him, and he likely had the same for her. She'd even taken the baptism a year ago, hoping it would prompt Jonas to take it and marry her, but he hadn't. He'd dragged his heels for the past year, and now his baptism was to take place tomorrow, and she didn't believe he intended to take it. If he didn't, he would not be able to marry her without her being shunned.

It was obvious Ellie had not taken the baptism either, and the two of them could be married immediately with no complications or repercussions to either of them within the community. They would not be able to be an active part of the community, but they would not be shunned from communication with other members. Knowing this did not help matters in her mind.

Was it right for her to stand in the way of her friend's happiness? Knowing how much Ellie loved Jonas, how could she? But what about her life, and her dreams, and her happiness?

"*Gott*, am I being selfish?"

Hannah had gotten so caught up with the idea of being married and having a *boppli* of her own, that she'd lost sight of what was right and wrong. Was she determined to have Jonas for her husband no matter what it cost her? Was she really willing to lose her friendship with Ellie?

At last, she reached her own driveway and dragged her feet up the grassy path. She didn't like walking in the dirt where the buggy wheels had worn off the grass, as she often twisted her ankles in the ruts in the path. But the grassy area did not come without obstacles that the horses had left behind, requiring her utmost attention along the way.

Lost in thought, she stepped with both feet into a large pile of fresh manure. Looking down at her soiled feet, she began to cry. She stomped her feet in the dirt, wiping them and scraping them to no avail. She stomped angrily all the way up to the porch of her house. Slipping out of her shoes, she stomped up the wooden steps of the porch, walked through the door, slamming it behind her.

Hannah ran up the stairs and into her room, letting the door slam behind her, and then flung herself across her bed, sobbing. Too many thoughts rolled around in her head. She had missed Ellie all this time, and would have wanted to share her wedding plans with her. But the fact of the matter was, she couldn't share them with her, because she was taking away the man whom her friend loved. All that time she'd spent grooming Jonas to be her husband had all been in vain. If she'd paid better attention, she would have noticed he didn't love her enough to marry her, but was simply going through the motions just as she was.

Was it right for the two of them to force a marriage where there was no love? A marriage of convenience could only end up in disaster, especially when they both loved Ellie so much. She'd lost her friend and her betrothed long before today, and it hurt her to realize the truth.

She turned her head from her pillow where she'd had it buried, and noticed her wedding dress hung over the chair in the corner of her room. She pushed herself from her bed and walked over to the dress, lifting it from the chair and pulling it to her cheek. She'd sewn that dress with so much care and so much hope, and now all that hope was gone. She clenched the dress in her fists, and in a rage of anger, tore the dress in two.

Shocked, and realizing what she'd done, she tossed the dress on the floor and flung herself back across her bed, sobbing even harder.

After several minutes, she wiped her eyes and began to pray.

Lord, please bless me with a peace in my heart if I'm to let Jonas go. If Katie is his kinner, take away the selfish thoughts I have of keeping that boppli away from her daed. Take away the fear I feel that I'll never have a husband or a boppli of my own, and replace it with a peace and trust that you'll work everything out with your plan for my life, and not my own. Restore my friendship with Ellie, and help me not to be bitter or envious. Put happiness in my heart for my two friends, deliver me from this anger and disappointment. Give me the patience to wait on you to provide a husband for me—the husband You would have for me. Please forgive me for trying to rule my own life when I know You are the ruler of my life and the universe. Danki, Lord, for all your many blessings, and bless Ellie with the courage to do what she needs to do for her familye. Give Jonas the courage to let me go and do what's right by his kinner. Give me strength, Gott, to let them be a familye. Give me strength, Gott, to let Your will be done in my life.

When she was finished, she felt a peace wash over her, and she knew it was time for her to step back and let it go. She would let God find her the husband he would have for her, and she would wait patiently for him.

Chapter 11

Jonas paced the barn floor, rehearsing what he would say to the two women he was now betrothed to. Hannah would likely never forgive him for changing his mind at the last minute, but he had to try with Ellie, even if it didn't work out in the end.

He would at least try.

As for the child she brought with her, he had thought deeply about that, and determined it didn't matter if all she needed was a father for her child. It was Ellie's flesh and blood, and he would help her raise her, and would gladly treat her like his own. Katie was a part of Ellie, so of course he would love her.

He stopped pacing for a moment, and faced the loft of the barn, leaning up against the post and reminiscing about that steamy afternoon before Ellie left the community. Was it possible that a child had resulted from that union? If so, why had she waited so long to return? Had she denied him the right to his own child this whole time? Hannah hadn't mentioned the age of the child, only that it was a girl and her name was Katie, but she had referred to her as a *boppli*. He did the math in his head, realizing that if he had fathered Katie, she would be approximately eighteen months old by now.

Suddenly, he was more eager than ever to find out the truth; he had to know if Katie belonged to him.

Removing his horse from his stall, Jonas harnessed him and then hitched him to the buggy. He still had plenty of chores to do, but he couldn't wait until later to speak with Ellie. After a failed attempt to talk to her last night, he realized it was a blessing in disguise, because it had given him time to think things through thoroughly.

He hopped in his buggy confident that a talk between him and Ellie was long overdue.

Driving down the lane, he contemplated whether or not he should finalize things with Hannah before he went to Ellie, but instead he said a little prayer for guidance.

Lord, I'm feeling confused, and angry, and betrayed. Help me to forgive Ellie for keeping Katie from me all this time if she is my kinner, and help me to understand her reasons. Help me to find my way through this mess without hurting anyone. Grant me peace about my decision to honor my commitment to Katie if she's my kinner and to Ellie, and forgive me for breaking the commitment with Hannah. Put

*forgiveness in Hannah's heart for me and help her to
realize we are not the right match. Forgive me,
Lord, for leading her to believe we should be
married when we're not equally yoked. Bless me
with favor in Ellie's eyes; Open the floodgates of
love between us if it is your will. Amen.*

By the time he finished his prayer, he was
steering his buggy into the lane of Ellie's family
home. As he neared the house, he could see Ellie
sitting on the porch with the child on her lap. From
what he could see, the little girl, with her blonde
curls that matched his own, was approximately the
age he'd guessed. Feelings of giddiness and
nervousness mixed in his stomach, making him feel
as if he wanted to run to the child, but yet turn away
at the same time for fear it wouldn't be true. Was he
ready for this?

He parked his buggy, unable to take his eyes
from the child. Her blue eyes that mirrored his own
sparkled in the late afternoon sun, and her little smile
was almost intoxicating. A warm feeling in his heart
traveled to the lump in his throat bringing tears to his
eyes. He hopped down from the buggy and stood
there for a moment just to take her into his heart.
Even from that distance, he could see that Katie was
his flesh and blood.

He walked swiftly to the porch steps and Ellie
put the child down from her lap. He flashed a quick
glance to Ellie as he reached the top step, and she
released her grip on the child. Little Katie ran to

greet Jonas, and he scooped her up in his arms, holding her close, tears flowing from his eyes. His lower lip quivered, despite the smile he could not wipe from his lips.

"Without a doubt, this has to be the best feeling in the world," he said.

He twirled the child around happily, and she giggled. "That's my girl," he said. "That's my girl."

Nothing else mattered to him at this moment, only the love he had for his child. There was a bond there that no amount of time or distance could steal away from him. He would never let anything stand between the two of them again. Not pride, which had kept him from going after Ellie when he should have. Not his standing in the community, which had torn him away from Ellie in the first place. But most assuredly, not his empty commitment to Hannah. His only commitment now would be to his child and her mother whom he loved dearly.

"*Danki,* Lord, for opening my eyes to the truth."

Jonas looked at Ellie, who waited patiently for him to come to terms. He adjusted little Katie in one arm, and extended his other to the woman he loved. She went to him easily without saying a word, and he pulled her close, tilting his head affectionately against hers.

All at once he realized he had everything he wanted and needed right there in his arms, and nothing else mattered. He would love them, and shelter them, and take care of them for as long as he lived. In doing this, he would fulfill the only commitment that mattered, and that was the one to his family and to God.

Chapter 12

The familiar sound of clip-clops and grinding wheels in the gravel driveway alerted Jonas to a buggy coming up behind him. He turned, keeping hold of his new family, his heart skipping a beat when he saw it was Hannah.

It was time to take care of the mess he'd created, and try to fix whatever he could, and let go of what he couldn't. He could do no more or no less.

Ellie tensed in his arms, and then lifted her head from his shoulder. "I'm not sure I'm ready for this visit."

"Let me take care of it," he whispered into her hair.

She would gladly let him handle his own dispute with Hannah, but she was her friend too, and Ellie didn't like being at odds with her. Truth was, she'd missed Hannah, and had often wished she could talk to her over the past couple of years since she'd been gone. They'd always confided everything in each other, and she'd kept so much bottled inside all this time, she felt deprived of the closeness they once shared. She'd confided some in her cousin while she was living there, but they weren't close enough that Ellie felt free to burden her with everything.

Hannah had always been such a good listener, that Ellie would often go on for hours about things she wanted to do when they grew up. She'd talked her ear off about her future plans, and how smooth her life was going to be once she was old enough to be on her own—and now look at her. Here she was, shaking in her shoes on the porch of her parent's home, and trying not to lose her temper over Hannah's unannounced invasion. Granted, her own sins had gotten her into the mess she was in, but now, she needed to rely on Jonas to stand strong with her while she worked her way out of it.

Hannah remained in the buggy, observing Jonas holding Katie. Seeing the two of them together, there was no doubt in her mind she was his flesh and blood. She took in a deep breath and released if slowly, as if letting go. Peace filled her heart, and she knew at that moment Jonas was exactly where he was meant to be, and God had something else in store for her future. But for the time-being, she had two friends waiting for her on the porch of the Yoder farm, and she was not going to let anything separate them again if she could help it.

Ellie had made her an *aenti,* even though they weren't related, they'd always been as close as two sisters could be, and they'd promised each other long before Katie was even a glint in Ellie's eye that they would always be *familye.*

They'd always planned to be married at the same time and they were going to raise their *kinner* together. They had done everything from pick out the names of their children, to deciding how many of each they would have. Always in that picture, Ellie was the one to marry Jonas—not Hannah.

Lord, bless me with renewed strength to put aside the envy I feel and step aside so that Ellie and Jonas can raise Katie together and be a familye. Put joy in my heart for the two of them, and bless me with the strength to support their future in any way I can.

Bless me, Lord, with a Jonas of my own...

Her thoughtful prayer trailed off as she felt in her heart that God was telling her to be patient and wait for the reward He had for her to repay her for the unselfish act she was about to perform. She felt at peace as she exited the buggy, fully intending to release Jonas from his commitment to her.

Jonas and Ellie walked down the steps and toward the buggy with welcoming smiles. Hannah ran to her friend, pulling her close.

"I'm so sorry for getting in the way of your rightful future with Jonas," she said to Ellie. "I've not been a *gut* friend, but I pray you'll still let me be Katie's *aenti.*"

Jonas and Ellie looked at each other, Hannah's comments taking them both by surprise. But they were of one mind where their friend, Hannah, was concerned.

"*Jah,*" Ellie said. "You'll always be *mei schweschder*—and Katie's *aenti.*"

"I've missed you so much, Ellie," Hannah said, tears filling her eyes, but her mouth formed a smile so wide, her heart overflowed with happiness for her friend and sister. "I wasn't sure if you'd ever be happy enough to want to come back home."

Ellie gave her a squeeze. "I am now!"

"*Wilkum* home."

Chapter 13

Hannah slipped inside the front door with *Frau* Yoder, allowing Ellie and Jonas a little quiet time alone. Once inside the house, *Frau* Yoder put her arm around Hannah and hugged her tight. "Are you all right?"

"*Jah*, I'm all right. It wasn't meant to be with me and Jonas. It wasn't part of *Gott's* plan for my life, and I know that now."

"I'm certain that *Gott* has another husband for you out there somewhere," *Frau* Yoder said. "I'm sure glad that you made up with Ellie. I've missed you. What do you say we go into the kitchen and finish the *familye* dinner?"

"But I don't want to interrupt your *familye* dinner. This is Ellie's homecoming, and I'm guessing it will be her engagement dinner as well."

"Don't you know by now that you're *familye* too, Hannah?"

"*Danki*. I have really missed working in this kitchen with you."

Hannah smiled. She certainly missed spending time in the kitchen with Ellie's mother. After Ellie left the community, Hannah had spent a lot of time with her mother. She missed having a mother around, and Ellie's mother had filled a void for her. When she began pursuing Jonas, she'd stopped visiting with the woman. She'd felt guilty for going over there while she was pursuing the woman's daughter's betrothed. She was certain the woman knew what she was up to anyway, which made it more difficult for her to face her.

To Hannah it was easier to stay away than to face the truth about what she was doing. Realistically, she was betraying her friend by showing interest in her betrothed. She would no longer have to be ashamed for what she did since she stepped aside and did the right thing by Ellie and Jonas, and even little Katie.

Though her wedding day was to be in two days, Hannah felt a sense of peace despite the fact she was no longer getting married. The peace that she now found would serve as a reminder that God was answering her prayer, and would bring her the right man to be her husband.

She washed her hands and set to work rolling up dough-balls to make rolls. She listened to Ellie's mother humming happily, and mentally went over the eligible man in the community. There were only two men, one was way too young for her, and the other was way too old. What was she to do? Perhaps her dad would agree to send her to another community to reside with one of her cousins where there might be some eligible men there. It was likely her only chance to find a husband. She would certainly pray about it, but already, she'd nearly made up her mind. There was nothing more for her here. Though she was happy that she'd made amends with Ellie, she didn't believe she could easily stay around and watch her friend have a life with the man she was supposed to marry. She wanted very much to put the bitterness behind her, and she wasn't sure she would be able to do that if she stayed too close to home.

Hannah and Ellie's *mamm* worked side-by-side in silence in the kitchen just like they always did. Occasionally, her *mamm* would tell her funny little stories about when Ellie was little, or Hannah would talk to her about missing her friend, but other than that, not much was ever said. They seemed to have an unspoken bond that didn't require a lot of conversation, and that usually suited Hannah just fine. It gave her a chance to have a bond with a motherly figure, without making a commitment or betraying her *mamm's* memory.

Before long, Hannah could hear Jonas and Ellie entering the house and it seemed Lydia and Eli were with them. The noise in the house had suddenly increased and *Frau* Yoder wiped her hands hastily on her apron and smiled excitedly.

"Everyone is here, Hannah," she said. "Let's go greet everyone."

"*Nee,*" Hannah said, shaking her head. "I'll finish up in here; you go and greet your son and his *fraa.*"

Before long, Lydia entered the kitchen and smiled at Hannah. She placed her hand over her enlarged abdomen.

"It won't be long before you're helping me bring this wee one into the world," she said with a smile.

Hannah had forgotten that she had agreed to deliver Lydia's baby. She wasn't due for a least three more weeks, and Hannah had no idea how she would be able to stand staying here that long. She had already decided that she would stay with her cousins and leave immediately after Jonas married Ellie. Surely she could be gracious enough to stay for their wedding, but she could not stand by and watch them live a life that she was supposed to live. It would do well to help rid herself of the anger and the bitterness, and give her the peace she sought after.

Lydia put a hand on Hannah's shoulder. "I know this probably isn't the best time," she said. "But in light of your circumstances, I'd like to know if you'll agree to stay with me for the next few weeks until I deliver my *boppli.*"

She hadn't given such a thing much thought, but she supposed it would allow her to stay away from the rest of the community. Lydia's home was on the outskirts of the community, making it an easy place to hide out.

"Eli will set up the room across the hall for you, and I think being away for a couple of weeks might do you some *gut*. I could certainly use the help, and will pay you wages, as I have a feeling you intend to go visiting *familye* outside the community, am I correct in saying so?"

"*Jah,*" she said, forcing a smile. "If you need me to stay, then I'll stay until you deliver."

Lydia threw her arms around Hannah excitedly. "*Danki*, Hannah. I promise I will pay you well, and after I deliver, you can go wherever your heart leads you, but I have a feeling you're going to be all right."

Hannah prayed that her decision to stay with Lydia was God's will. If not, she had just agreed to do something else without consulting God first.

It would seem that listening to God and waiting on Him was going to be a hard lesson for Hannah to learn.

Chapter 14

Hannah tried her best to focus on conversation during dinner, and not allow the looks between Jonas and Ellie to bother her. She stuffed a bite of roast chicken in her mouth hoping it would divert her attention away from them and give her a moment to think without having to speak. She reminded herself that God had something else in store for her and silently begged God once again to take away any apprehension she had of her decision.

Would it always be this way? Or would she get to a point where it never bothered her again? At the moment, she didn't think so, but she supposed with time, like all wounds, it would heal.

There was no talk of the wedding, and Hannah thought that it was probably awkward for Jonas and Ellie to be around her right now. She suddenly wished that she hadn't accepted the invitation to dinner, knowing that she was keeping them from making their plans. She had to assume that they wanted to marry as soon as possible before

Lydia gave birth so that she would not be still recovering after the pregnancy and unable to attend.

At the conclusion of the meal, Hannah began to clear the table. She just couldn't sit there any longer, and she didn't know what to do with herself. Keeping her hands busy was all she could do, and clearing the table would keep her mind busy too.

Ellie followed her into the kitchen, setting down the single plate she'd grabbed as an excuse to tag along behind her. She set the plate down and turned to Hannah, trying not to let discouragement set in.

From the other room, Hannah could hear little Katie giggling where she sat bouncing on Jonas's lap. Her focus turned back to Ellie, who was standing before her looking as though she wanted to say something.

"I'm sorry if this is hard for you," Ellie said. "The last thing I would ever want to do would be to make you feel uncomfortable."

Hannah turned on the water in the sink and squirted some soap in to start some dishwater. With her back to Ellie, she took a deep breath and pushed it out slowly to keep her tone cheery. "I'm not sure it can be helped. The situation sort of calls for it, don't you think?"

Ellie put the plate into the dishwater and then leaned her back against the counter. "I suppose you've got me there. But our friendship means so much to me and I want so much to include you in our plans."

"*Ach*, you don't want me tagging along. I'd be a third wheel. Besides, I was courting Jonas, so why would you want me to attend your wedding?"

"Because you're my friend above anything else!"

Hannah scoffed. "How does Jonas feel about that? I'm certain he doesn't want to be reminded that I nearly talked him into marrying me so easily."

She'd lost that quest, and she fought hard to push back envy for her friend. She reminded herself that she would have faith that God would bring her the right man to marry, and that Jonas was not that man for many reasons, little Katie being the biggest one.

"He doesn't hold anything against you," Ellie said. "If that's what you mean."

Hannah sighed heavily as she stared out the kitchen window, washing a plate mindlessly. Winter would be here soon enough, and another Christmas would pass her by without a husband. She had hoped that this would be the year that she would not go through another set of holidays alone. Granted, she had her sister, Rachel, but her dad had been too quiet since their *mamm* had died almost two years ago. Ellie hadn't even been here for her for that.

Instead, Jonas had been the one to get her through those hard times. And for that she would always be grateful for his friendship. But looking back on it, that's all it had ever been between the two of them. They hadn't even shared a kiss, making the excuse to one another that they would wait until their wedding. She had fooled herself into thinking that day would ever come.

As if she knew what Hannah was thinking, Ellie placed a hand on her shoulder thoughtfully. "I wanted to tell you how sorry I was to hear about your *mamm*. But I'm glad that Jonas was there for you."

"How did you know I was thinking about her just now?"

Ellie looked at Hannah seriously. "Because we're friends and we've always been connected that way."

Hannah smiled. "You always did seem to be able to look right through my soul."

"Maybe because you've always been so transparent. I knew when I saw you yesterday that you weren't really in love with Jonas so much as the idea of being married. It was all you ever talked about when we were younger. You were the one that wanted to be married more than I ever did. And here I am the one taking that leap of faith. But don't worry, because I know *Gott* has a wonderful husband in store for you, one that will love you and cherish you for the rest of your days. And you'll have lots and lots of *kinner*."

Hannah's face brightened. "Do you really think so, Ellie?"

"Of course I do, and to show you just how confident I am about that, I'd like it if you'd stand with me at my wedding," Ellie said. "I'll be married in the Mennonite church since we won't be able to be married by the bishop. Since neither of us has taken the baptism, being married in the Mennonite church is the only logical solution for us right now. But I'd really like you to stand with me when I get married."

"You mean like a maid of honor at an *Englisch* wedding?"

"Yes, exactly like that."

Hannah paused for just a moment, and there it was; the peace that she'd been asking God for.

She smiled. "*Jah*, I'd like that very much."

Chapter 15

Eli hugged his twin sister tightly. "I'm proud of you, Ellie, for enduring what you had to in order to bring little Katie into this world. I only wish you would have brought her home sooner than this so we could've gotten to know her a little better. Seeing her makes me even more eager to be a *vadder*."

A lump formed in Ellie's throat, guilt threatening to overtake her. She hadn't wanted to be so secretive where little Katie was concerned, but she just hadn't been certain what would be waiting for her back home when others found out she was an unwed mother. It helped to ease her fears knowing that her family was so close with her and supported all the surprising changes that had taken place since she got home. She hadn't expected the kind of support they were giving her, or even the drastic change with her relationship with Jonas. All she knew was that she would no longer have to be shameful, for she would no longer be an unwed mother.

"Thank you, Eli, it means a lot to me that you support me and Jonas."

He smiled. "All too soon, me and Lydia will have a *boppli* of our own, and Katie will have a new cousin."

"Did you want me to come over and help with the delivery?" Ellie asked.

"*Nee*, Lydia has made arrangements with Hannah to stay with us for the remaining days until the birth. And since she's taken over being the midwife for her *mamm*, we have every confidence in her. But we would love for you to be there too. We're nervous, and we can use all the support we can get."

It surprised her that Hannah would agree to such a thing, but she supposed now that her plans with Jonas had abruptly ended, she needed a distraction, and staying so far out of the community would probably be good for Hannah right now. She'd left quietly more than a half-hour ago, or Ellie would have gone to her and made sure that she was all right with this. She supposed it would be a while before she could totally mend fences with Hannah, and things might be strange and awkward for a while, but she hoped it wouldn't be for long.

"Of course we'll be there," Ellie promised. "We'll check in with you as often as we can over the next few days. And if things happen sooner, please send word so that we can be there."

The two of them hugged tightly as Lydia exited the house with their *mamm*. Eli gave his *mamm* a good strong hug, and then wrapped his arm around his wife and held her hand as he assisted her down the stairs and into their buggy. Once he had his wife situated, he turned to wave, and then turned his buggy around so they could go home.

Jonas, who was carrying Katie on his hip, caught up with Ellie on the porch just in time to wave goodbye to his soon-to-be brother and sister-in-law. He handed Katie over to Ellie's *mamm* so the two of them could have some quiet time on the porch and watch the sunset together. He placed a hand at the small of Ellie's back, guiding her to the porch swing at the end of the porch.

"Do you want to take the baptism?" He asked.

She shrugged. "I thought a lot about it, but I would have to take the classes, and that would delay our wedding. Did you still intend to take the baptism tomorrow?"

He shook his head. "I've been dragging my heels all this time, not wanting to take the baptism unless you did. If I took the baptism, you and I would be unequally yoked. I want to be married first, so we don't delay our being a *familye* any longer. We can discuss the baptism later, unless you're determined to take it beforehand."

She shook her head as well. "I won't take it unless you do. But we can discuss that later, I suppose. Right now, all I want to do is be married to you and be a *familye* with Katie. I believe the rest will take care of itself. I've talked to *mei familye* about it, and they're not requiring it of me at this point. And since we won't be under the rules of our community, we won't be shunned."

"I agree," she said with a smile.

"Then it's settled," he said. "I'll make arrangements with the Mennonite preacher."

"*Jah*, I can't wait to be married to you."

He smiled, feeling happier and more at peace than he'd been in a couple of years. "I love you, Ellie."

Warmth filled her from the top of her head all the way down to her toes, making her feel as giddy as she had when they were younger and so much in love. She knew that her love for him had never wavered. Now, nothing would stand in the way of their happiness and their future together as a family.

"I love you too, Jonas."

He pulled her close, love and renewed passion filling him so much, that he couldn't help but press his lips to hers. He swept his lips across hers, and over to her cheek, then, down her neck, following the trail back up to her ear where he whispered to her how much he loved her. She closed her eyes, enjoying the closeness with him so much she hadn't realized a buggy had approached in the driveway.

Before either of them realized, and angry male voice was interrupting they're passionate kisses.

Jonas pulled away from Ellie, and stood up to greet Hannah's father.

"Why have you dishonored my *dochder* by kissing Ellie when you're betrothed to my Hannah?"

Jonas cleared his throat, and took a deep breath to calm his racing heart. His hands shook, and a bead of sweat formed on his forehead. He hadn't put much thought into having to give an explanation to her father, but he supposed it was the right thing, and he should've done it long before now.

"I'm no longer betrothed to Hannah," he said cautiously. "I'm going to marry Ellie."

"When she tried telling me that you had called off the wedding, I had to come and see for myself. I had no idea this is what I would find—you kissing her best friend. You have shamed my daughter, and now she will be a spinster because of you."

Jonas felt guilty enough for the way he'd handled the situation with Hannah, but the words of her father stung.

The angry man turned his attention to Ellie, who had remained on the porch-swing with her eyes cast downward. "And you, Ellie, you're supposed to be her friend. How could you betray her in this way?"

Ellie's heart skipped a beat. Had Hannah gone home and embellished the situation with her father in order to save-face with him? Surely she would have had to explain things differently to her strict father who wouldn't have understood the way Hannah claimed she had. Or perhaps Hannah had been hurt far more than either of them had noticed. Had they been caught up so far in their own desires that they had lost sight of the hurt they'd caused Hannah?

"It was never my intention to break up the wedding between Jonas and Hannah, but Jonas and I have a child together, and because of that we intend to marry."

His jaw clenched and his eyes narrowed. "My Hannah told me that the two of you have a *boppli*, and I think it's a shame to the community what you have done. I don't want you to have anything more to do with my *dochder*. As far as I'm concerned you're no longer a part of her life, and you are no longer friends because you've not acted like one."

"I mean no disrespect," Jonas said. "But we will always be friends with Hannah."

"*Nee*," he said. "You may not be shunned as far as the bishop is concerned, but as for *mei haus* and *mei familye*, you're shunned."

He walked down the steps of the porch and jumped in his buggy, driving off before either of them could gather their wits about them enough to say another word. It was probably for the best right now, that they allow him time to adjust and calm down. They had both been raised not to argue with their elders, and for now, Jonas would let the matter drop.

Ellie began to cry. "I want Hannah to be at our wedding," she sobbed. "She promised me she would stand with me as a maid of honor."

Jonas pulled her close. "I'm sorry, my dear Ellie, but we might be on our own for a while. I'm sure our decision and the news of Katie will shock the entire community. It might be a while before we have their support, and it's possible, that we may never have it."

Ellie sobbed even harder. She had thought by marrying Jonas that everything in her life would fall into the proper places, but it was apparent that they had not. Hannah's father was an important and respected man in the community, and his anger could change everything for them. She didn't want their decision and their mistakes to cause her family to be shunned because of it, and Hannah's father had that power.

Chapter 16

Ellie paced the length of the room off the side of the little Mennonite chapel where she was readying herself to meet Jonas at the altar.

Lord, Hannah promised she'd be here to stand up with me. Please allow her safe passage to be here. I don't want to be married without my best friend here.

A quiet knock sounded at the door, and Ellie rushed to open it.

"Ach, it's only you!" she said to her twin brother.

"Danki for the warm *wilkum,"* Eli complained.

She pulled him into a hug. "I'm sorry; I was hoping you were Hannah."

"Did I hear my name?"

Ellie's face lit up as her friend walked in the room. She threw her arms around her and began to cry. "I'm so happy you're here! I didn't want to get married without you here."

"Ach, I wouldn't have made it if it weren't for the fact *mei daed* had agreed to let me move in with your *bruder* and his *fraa* today. *Danki* for arranging that for me, by the way," she said, directing the last part to Eli.

"I'm glad I could help in any way," he said. "Besides, Lydia is eager for you to be there. She's been anxious; worrying you wouldn't be there on time to deliver the wee one."

Hannah giggled. "Every woman goes through that in their last few days," she assured him. "It's nothing to be alarmed about. I'm all packed, so after the wedding, I can take my things to your *haus.*"

"Lydia will be pleased to know that," he said.

"I saw her out in the hall before I came in here, and told her the news already, so she's breathing a little more calmly now."

Hannah began to fuss with the collar on Ellie's dress to smooth out the crisp, white linen, which was a nice compliment to the traditional blue of her dress. It seemed odd to her that Ellie would choose the color even though she wasn't being married by the bishop, but she didn't pry. She could only assume the two of them intended on taking the baptism after they were married. She would have to remember to ask her about it later, but for now, it was time to get her ready to walk down that aisle to meet Jonas.

Hannah took one last look at her. "You're a beautiful bride, Ellie."

"*Danki,* Hannah, but you know you're next!"

Hannah scoffed at her. "I'm not so sure about that."

Eli kissed her forehead. "I agree with *mei schweschder,* Hannah. You're a beautiful person, and any *mann* will consider himself lucky to have you as his *fraa.*"

His comment and affection surprised Hannah, but they'd all known each other their entire lives, and she and Eli used to kiss behind the barn; there had been a time when they were much younger that Hannah had thought she would marry her best friend's twin brother so they could be sisters, but it hadn't worked out that way.

Lydia had come to the community to live with her grandmother and take care of her in her last days, and Eli had become smitten with her from the moment he met her.

After that day, their childhood crush ended.

Hannah thought it funny how naïve they had been when they were younger, and she suddenly wished for those days back, but they were all grown up now. Maybe, just maybe, they were a little too grown up.

Chapter 17

Hannah watched Jonas kissing his new bride, and couldn't help but wonder what it would have been like to be standing right where Ellie was right now. She glanced back at Eli and Lydia and wondered the same thing. She'd passed up two opportunities to be married, and now she was going to be residing in the home of one of them. It was tough not to be envious, but she had to remind herself for the millionth time today that God had another plan for her future. She would likely be spending a lot of time in prayer and reminding herself of his plan for her life over the next several weeks. She had determined to leave the community to go stay with her cousins after the birth of Lydia's baby. There was just too much history here in this community and it was all too close to home. She needed to be free from the past in order to move forward in her future.

No matter how many times she tried to tell herself that it was a temporary situation, she couldn't shake the feeling it was going to turn into a permanent one. No matter how many times she put it out of her head, she just couldn't see a life outside of this community, no matter how much she tried to envision it and plan for it. Regardless of whatever it was that was in her way, she would continue to believe it was the right plan even though God always seemed to have a way of changing her plans on her.

Once outside the church, Hannah walked toward her buggy, but Ellie called after her. She stopped and waited for Ellie to catch up to her even though she couldn't get away from the scene fast enough. Although she wasn't eager to be settling into Eli's house with him and his wife, it was the best solution all-around.

"I wanted to thank you for being with me today, Hannah," she said a little out of breath. "Even though I know how tough it must've been for you. I appreciate the sacrifice more than you know."

"I was happy to do it. But I'm afraid I must go and get myself settled into your *bruder's haus*. I'll come back after unpacking so I can help your *mamm* serve your guests."

Ellie pulled Hannah into a hug, thinking how sorry she was for putting her through all of this. She's been a gracious friend to endure all of this, and she said a little prayer that God would bring her a husband of her own very soon.

Ellie released her friend, and Hannah knew she'd been praying for her. Not only could she feel the blessings pouring down, but she knew by her friend's silence that she was deep in prayer.

They parted ways, and Hannah knew without a doubt that everything was going to work out just the way God planned it.

As she drove away from the church, she resisted the temptation to look back. Her future was not there, it was somewhere out in front of her, and she was more than ready to get there and settle into it—in God's timing.

Chapter 18

After the last wedding guest had left, Jonas turned to his bride and whispered in her ear. "Are you ready to go home?"

She had been so caught up in everything that she hadn't really given it a thought, but she was eager to see the home she would be living in with her new husband. He'd casually mentioned he had a place of his own, and she was certainly ready to begin her life with him.

They packed up Katie, despite her *mamm's* offer to keep her for the night. As parents, they knew it would be best to get her settled into her new home as quickly as possible to avoid adding anymore uncertainty to the already stressful changes that the child had endured. She'd been very content with the move so far, and they hoped the transition to their final home would be an easy one for her.

Ellie had already packed their things, and Jonas had gotten the crib his *daed* had made for him and placed it in the room across the hall from the master bedroom. He'd thought of everything, and it had given Ellie a chance to concentrate only on the wedding itself.

As they pulled into a long driveway almost directly behind her family farm, Ellie was happy to know that she would be living so close to her *mamm,* whom she'd mentioned to Jonas she'd needed to keep an eye on. He'd agreed, and had assured her his farm was very close; she hadn't realized it would be this close, and she was pleased.

As they neared the house, Ellie looked at a large, two-story farmhouse with a wraparound porch against the backdrop of a large pond. The moon shone on the water, lighting up the heavily-wooded property. Her breath caught in her throat at the beauty of her new home. When Jonas pulled the buggy in front of the porch, happy tears filled her eyes. It was just as they'd talked about; the home they would build when they married.

Jonas noticed Ellie being so emotional.

"I built the *haus* from memory; I hope I got everything just the way you wanted."

She giggled, letting out a joyful cry. "It's perfect!"

"It should be," he said, leaning in and kissing her damp cheek. "I built it just for you."

Ellie pushed the thought from her mind that her own stubbornness had almost caused another woman—Hannah, to live in the home that Jonas had built for her.

None of that mattered now. They had both grown up today, and done the right thing—by each other and their daughter.

He assisted her out of the buggy; Katie was sleeping soundly in her arms.

Once on the porch, Jonas scooped both of them up in his arms and carried them into the house. He let her down easily, so as not to wake his daughter.

He kissed Ellie and smiled. *"Wilkum* home!"

She giggled as she looked around the house he'd built with love, feeling that she had finally found her way back home.

THE END

Look for book 2 in this series…

Please enjoy the sneak preview chapter of
Amish Suspense, The Amish Girl: Book One

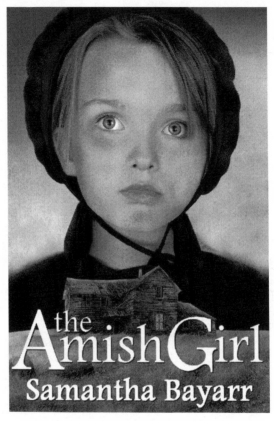

The Amish Girl

Samantha Jillian Bayarr

A note from the Author:

While this novel is set against the backdrop of an Amish community, the characters and the names of the community are fictional. There is no intended resemblance between the characters in this book or the setting, and any real members of any Amish or Mennonite community. As with any work of fiction, I've taken license in some areas of research as a means of creating the necessary circumstances for my characters and setting. It is completely impossible to be accurate in details and descriptions, since every community differs, and such a setting would destroy the fictional quality of entertainment this book serves to present. Any inaccuracies in the Amish and Mennonite lifestyles portrayed in this book are completely due to fictional license. Please keep in mind that this book is meant for fictional, entertainment purposes only, and is not written as a text book on the Amish.

Happy Reading

Chapter 1

Ten-year-old Amelia bolted upright in bed, her heart racing from the crack of lightning that split the air on such a quiet, summer night. The crickets' song had suddenly stopped, and all she could hear was the muffled sound of her own heart beating.

Tilting her head to listen, her eyes bulged in the dark room as she tried to focus. The pale moonlight filtered in through the thin curtains beside her bed, a gentle breeze fluttering the sheers against the sill. Outside her window, the cornstalks in the field swayed, flapping their leaves with a familiar rhythm.

It smelled like rain was on the way.

She sucked in a ragged breath, her exhale catching as if she was out of air. Her heart beat faster still, fear flowing through her veins like ice water. A bead of sweat ran down her back between her shoulder blades, causing her to shiver.

Had she been dreaming?

Scooting to the edge of the bed, her legs felt a little wobbly as she let her feet down easy against the cool, wood floor. It was a comfort on such a warm night, though it increased her risk of wetting her pants.

She reached for the door handle, but pulled her hand away, the hair on the back of her neck prickling a warning. Tip-toeing back to her bed, she climbed in under the quilt, crossing her legs and leaning on her haunches to keep from wetting herself.

An unfamiliar voice carried from the other room, causing her heart to race and her limbs to tremble. It was an angry voice.

Another shot rent the air. It was the same noise that had woken her.

Her mother cried out, calling her father's name.

"*Mamm,*" Amelia whispered into the night air.

Once again, she pushed back the light quilt, her need to see her mother forcing her wobbly legs to support her tiny frame. Moving slowly, she made sure to be quiet, cringing every time the floor planks creaked.

It was unlike her parents to be so loud in the middle of the night, but something was terribly wrong.

Wondering who belonged to the mysterious voice, she listened to him arguing with her mother. Her voice was shaky, like she was crying, and it frightened Amelia.

"We don't have any money," her mother cried. "Please don't do this!"

Where was her father, and where had the other man come from? Who was this man, and why was he upsetting her mother? She peeked around the corner from the hallway, spotting a man dressed in black, with a gun raised and pointed at her mother.

Amelia shook, and her teeth chattered uncontrollably.

A single lantern flickered from the table, her eyes darted around the dimly-lit room, trying to place her father. She pulled in another ragged breath when she spotted him lying on the floor, blood pooling around his head. The noise that had woken her hadn't been in her dreams, it was the gunshot that had killed her father.

Every instinct in her warned her to hide, but her feet seemed unwilling to take her back to her room.

"This is your last chance," the gunman warned. "If you won't give me my money, you lose your life!"

"No!" she screamed. "Please, I don't have it."

"I had to spend the last ten years in jail for nothing," the man said through gritted teeth. "While the two of you spent *my* money on this nice farmhouse, and all those acres you have out there? You've been enjoying your life all these years with your horses and chickens and such, while I've been locked away with nothing!"

He aimed the gun at her, and she dropped to the floor, crying and pleading with him to spare her life.

He ignored her pleas.

Amelia shook violently, her gasp masked by a second gunshot, killing her mother right before her eyes.

She let out a strangled cry, and the man holding the gun turned toward her, his eyes locking with hers for a moment.

"Well, now, isn't this a nice surprise!" he said, tilting his head back and laughing madly.

His laugh sent chills through her, causing her bladder to empty uncontrollably.

For a moment, Amelia was paralyzed with fear, her feet unmovable in the puddle of urine. Lightning lit up the room, a crash of thunder bringing her back to her senses.

She forced her feet to propel her forward, heaving them as if they were chained to the floor. Swinging open the back door, she ran toward the cornfield that separated them from the

Yoder farm. Glancing over her shoulder, she looked back to see the man was behind her, hobbling as if he had a lame leg.

"Don't run, little Amish girl," he called after her. "I'm not going to hurt you!"

She entered the cornfield, visualizing the path she took on a daily basis when she visited with Caleb, her neighbor and friend. She'd never come through it in the dark, and her mind was too cluttered with fear that ripped at her gut to follow the path. Bile rose in her throat, but she swallowed it down as she ran. Cornstalks whipped at her face and arms, her mind barely aware of the stings that meant they'd drawn blood.

She stumbled, her breath heaving, as she scrambled on her hands and knees long enough to right herself. Her bare feet painfully dug into the rocks and dirt in the field, but her instinct was to stay alive.

The small barn at the back edge of the Yoder property had been a meeting place for her and Caleb. A place where they'd played with the barn cats and their kittens, and washed their horses after a long ride. But most of all, it was a place she knew there was a gun. Caleb had taught her how to shoot it, using tin cans for practice, but she'd never thought to turn it on a human—until now.

The main house was still too far away. Amelia knew her only chance of surviving this man's fury was to surprise him with the unexpected. All she wanted was for him to leave her alone, and she didn't have the physical strength to run any further. Pointing a gun at him the way he'd pointed it at her mother was the only thing on her mind. It drove her to reach the barn before the man who intended to kill her.

All she could think about, as she ran faster than she'd ever run before, was getting her hands on the gun she knew was in the Yoder's barn. The gun would give her power—the power to stop this man from killing her. Neither her *mamm* nor her *daed* had a gun, and now they were dead—both of them. Amelia didn't want to die. It was one of her biggest fears in her short life, and right now, that fear drove her to stay alive at all cost.

She entered the barn out of breath, her eyes struggling to focus. If not for the large window near the tack room filtering in the flashes of lightning, she would not be able to find her way. Crawling under the workbench, Amelia grabbed for the strongbox that housed the gun. The lock on it had long-since been broken, but she shook so much, she struggled to pry open the rusted lid. A flicker of lightning revealed the Derringer inside the metal box, and she snatched it quickly, and cracked the barrel forward. She'd done it a hundred times before when she and Caleb practiced, not knowing she'd ever have to use it to defend herself.

Shoving her shaky hand inside the box of ammunition, she grabbed haphazardly, and then loaded two bullets. Gripping the small handgun, she aimed it toward the door, waiting for her stalker.

"Come out, come out, little Amish girl. I'm not going to hurt you," the man called out to her.

Amelia sucked in a breath and drew the loaded gun out in front of her, darting it back and forth until her eyes focused on her assailant. Lightning blinked him in and out of her sight.

She flinched when he struck a match and lit the lantern hanging up just inside the doorway, turning up the flame until it lit up the room.

Amelia stayed crouched down under the work bench in the tack room, gun extended in front of her. She held her breath when she saw the look in his eyes, and knew he meant to do her harm.

The man spotted Amelia's feet underneath the work bench and smiled widely, but it wasn't a kind smile. "Why are you pointing a gun at me?" he asked. "I'm not going to hurt you!"

Her entire body tensed up, fear making her grip on the gun grow tighter. She stared at him, breathing hard through clenched teeth, her hands shaky.

He laughed at her. "We both know you aren't going to shoot me."

She pulled back the hammer of the gun fast and sure, without taking her eyes off of him.

His hands went up in mock defense, but he laughed nervously. "This isn't funny, Amish girl. I put my gun away, but you better put that gun down before I have to hurt you!"

She raised the gun as he moved slowly toward her, keeping it trained on his heart. Though she only meant to intimidate him the way he was doing to her, she had no intention of pulling the trigger. Her aim was too accurate.

"Put the gun down, little Amish girl," he said through gritted teeth.

Thunder rumbled, making her jump as he lurched toward her.

She let out a scream as she accidentally squeezed the trigger, a single shot discharging with a puff of smoke from the end of the barrel. Her eyes closed against the explosion that rang in her ears like the crack of thunder from the oncoming storm. When the smoke cleared, she could see that the bullet had gone straight through the man's chest, and he'd collapsed to the ground in front of her.

She kept the gun trained on him, staring into his unblinking eyes; her hands shaking and her breath catching, as she strangled the whimpering that intermittently escaped her lips.

She hadn't meant to shoot him; hadn't meant to kill him, but now he was dead—just like her parents.

You might also like these titles…

Little Wild Flower Book 4

Amish Wildflowers Collection

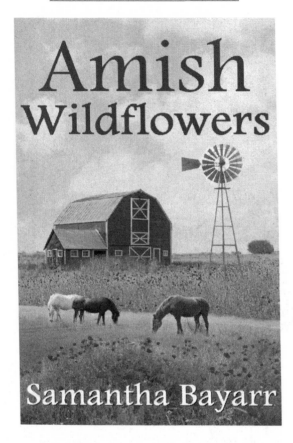

Amish Quilters

Amish Daughters

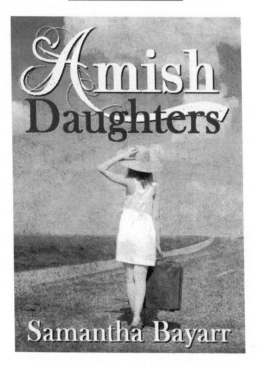

60847621R00071

Made in the USA
Lexington, KY
20 February 2017